VOCAL SCORE

OF

TRIAL BY JURY

BY

W. S. GILBERT

AND

ARTHUR SULLIVAN.

© International Music Publications Limited
Griffin House 161 Hammersmith Road
London W6 8BS, England

TRIAL BY JURY

Characters.

The Learned Judge.

The Plaintiff.

The Defendant.

Counsel for the Plaintiff.

Usher.

Foreman of the Jury.

Associate.

First Bridesmaid.

Bridesmaids. Gentlemen of the Jury,

Barristers, Attorneys, and Public.

Time of performance, three-quarters of an hour.

TRIAL BY JURY

SCENE.—*A Court of Justice. The Bench faces the audience, and extends along the back of the Court. The Judge's desk* C., *with canopy overhead, Jury-box* R., *Counsel's seats* L. *Barristers, Attorneys, Jurymen and Public discovered.*

CHORUS.

Hark, the hour of ten is sounding ;
Hearts with anxious fears are bounding,
Hall of Justice crowds surrounding,
 Breathing hope and fear—
For to-day in this arena,
Summoned by a stern subpœna,
Edwin, sued by Angelina,
 Shortly will appear.

Enter USHER.

SOLO—USHER.

Now, Jurymen, hear my advice—
All kinds of vulgar prejudice
 I pray you set aside :
With stern judicial frame of mind,
From bias free of every kind,
 This trial must be tried !

CHORUS.

From bias free of every kind,
This trial must be tried.

(*During Chorus,* USHER *sings fortissimo,* "*Silence in Court !*")

USHER.

Oh, listen to the plaintiff's case :
Observe the features of her face—
 The broken-hearted bride.
Condole with her distress of mind :
From bias free of every kind,
 This trial must be tried !

CHORUS.

From bias free, &c.

USHER.

And when amid the plaintiff's shrieks,
The ruffianly defendant speaks—
 Upon the other side ;
What *he* may say you needn't mind—
From bias free of every kind,
 This trial must be tried !

CHORUS.

From bias free, &c.

Enter DEFENDANT L.

RECIT.—DEFENDANT.

Is this the Court of the Exchequer ?

ALL.

It is !

DEFENDANT (*aside*).

Be firm, be firm, my pecker,
Your evil star's in the ascendant !

ALL.

Who are you ?

DEFENDANT.

I'm the Defendant !

Chorus of JURYMEN (*shaking their fists*).

Monster, dread our damages.
 We're the jury,
 Dread our fury !

DEFENDANT.

Hear me, hear me, if you please,
 These are very strange proceedings—
For permit me to remark
 On the merits of my pleadings,
You're at present in the dark.

(DEFENDANT *beckons to* JURYMEN—*they leave the box and gather round him as they sing the following*) :—

That's a very true remark—
 On the merits of his pleadings,
We're at present in the dark !
 Ha ! ha !—ho ! ho !

SONG—DEFENDANT.

When first my old, old love I knew,
 My bosom welled with joy :
My riches at her feet I threw—
 I was a love-sick boy !
No terms seemed too extravagant
 Upon her to employ—
I used to mope, and sigh, and pant,
 Just like a love-sick boy !
  Tink-a-Tank—Tink-a-Tank.

But joy incessant palls the sense ;
 And love unchanged will cloy,
And she became a bore intense
 Unto her love-sick boy !
With fitful glimmer burnt my flame,
 And I grew cold and coy,
At last, one morning, I became
 Another's love-sick boy.
  Tink-a-Tank—Tink-a-Tank.

Chorus of JURYMEN (*advancing stealthily*).

Oh, I was like that when a lad !
 A shocking young scamp of a rover,
I behaved like a regular cad ;
 But that sort of thing is all over.
I am now a respectable chap
 And shine with a virtue resplendent,
And, therefore, I haven't a rap
 Of sympathy with the defendant !
  He shall treat us with awe,
  If there isn't a flaw,
Singing so merrily—Trial-la-law !
Trial-la-law—Trial-la-law !
Singing so merrily— Trial-la-law !

(*They enter the jury-box.*)

RECIT.—USHER (*on Bench*).

Silence in Court, and all attention lend.
Behold your Judge ! In due submission bend !

Enter JUDGE *on bench.*

CHORUS.

All hail great Judge !
 To your bright rays,
We never grudge
 Ecstatic praise.
  All hail !
May each decree
 As statute rank,
And never be
 Reversed in Banc.
  All hail !

RECIT.—JUDGE.

For these kind words accept my thanks, I pray,
A Breach of Promise we've to try to-day.
But firstly, if the time you'll not begrudge,
I'll tell you how I came to be a Judge.

ALL.

He'll tell us how he came to be a Judge.

JUDGE.

Let me speak, &c.

ALL.

Let him speak, &c.

SONG—JUDGE.

When I, good friends, was called to the bar,
    I'd an appetite fresh and hearty,
But I was, as many young barristers are,
    An impecunious party.
I'd a swallow-tail coat of a beautiful blue—
    A brief which I bought of a booby—
A couple of shirts and a collar or two,
    And a ring that looked like a ruby !

CHORUS.

A couple of shirts, &c.

JUDGE.

In Westminster Hall I danced a dance,
    Like a semi-despondent fury ;
For I thought I never should hit on a chance
    Of addressing a British Jury—
But I soon got tired of third-class journeys,
    And dinners of bread and water ;
So I fell in love with a rich attorney's
    Elderly, ugly daughter.

CHORUS.

So he fell in love, &c.

JUDGE.

The rich attorney, he jumped for joy,
    And replied to my fond professions :
"You shall reap the reward of your pluck, my boy,
    At the Bailey and Middlesex Sessions.
You'll soon get used to her looks," said he,
    "And a very nice girl you'll find her !
She may very well pass for forty-three
    In the dusk, with a light behind her !"

CHORUS.

She may very well, &c.

JUDGE.

The rich attorney was good as his word :
    The briefs came trooping gaily,
And every day my voice was heard
    At the Sessions or Ancient Bailey.
All thieves who could my fees afford
    Relied on my orations,
And many a burglar I've restored
    To his friends and his relations.

CHORUS.

And many a burglar, &c.

JUDGE.

At length I became as rich as the Gurneys—
    An incubus then I thought her,
So I threw over that rich attorney's
    Elderly, ugly daughter.
The rich attorney my character high
    Tried vainly to disparage—
And now, if you please, I'm ready to try
    This Breach of Promise of Marriage !

CHORUS.

And now, if you please, &c.

JUDGE.

For now I'm a Judge !

ALL.

And a good Judge too !

JUDGE.

Yes, now I'm a Judge !

ALL.

And a good Judge too !

JUDGE.

Though all my law be fudge,
Yet I'll never, never budge,
But I'll live and die a Judge.

ALL.

And a good Judge too !

JUDGE (*pianissimo*).
It was managed by a job—

ALL.

And a good job too !

JUDGE.

It was managed by a job !

ALL.

And a good job too !

JUDGE.

It is patent to the mob,
That my being made a nob
Was effected by a job.

ALL.

And a good job too !

Enter COUNSEL *for* PLAINTIFF. *He takes his place in front row of Counsels' seats.*

RECIT.—COUNSEL.
Swear thou the Jury !

USHER.

Kneel, Jurymen, oh, kneel !

(*All the* JURY *kneel in the Jury-box, and so are hidden from audience.*)

USHER.

Oh, will you swear by yonder skies,
    Whatever question may arise,
'Twixt rich and poor—'twixt low and high,
    That you will well and truly try.

JURY (*raising their hands, which alone are visible*).
    To all of this we make reply,
    By the dull slate of yonder sky :
    That we will well and truly try.

(*All rise with the last note.*)

RECIT.—COUNSEL.
Where is the plaintiff ?
Let her now be brought.

RECIT.—USHER.
Oh, Angelina ! Angelina ! ! Come thou into Court !

Enter the BRIDESMAIDS.

Chorus of BRIDESMAIDS.
Comes the broken flower—
    Comes the cheated maid—
Though the tempest lower,
    Rain and cloud will fade !
Take, oh maid, these posies :
    Though thy beauty rare
Shame the blushing roses—
    They are passing fair !
        Wear the flowers till they fade ;
        Happy be thy life, oh maid !

(*The* JUDGE, *having taken a great fancy to* 1ST BRIDESMAID, *sends her a note by* USHER, *which she reads, kisses rapturously, and places in her bosom.*)

Enter PLAINTIFF.

SOLO.—PLAINTIFF.
O'er the season vernal,
    Time may cast a shade ;
Sunshine, if eternal,
    Makes the roses fade :
Time may do his duty ;
    Let the thief alone—
Winter hath a beauty,
    That is all his own.
        Fairest days are sun and shade :
        I am no unhappy maid !

(The JUDGE having by this time transferred his admiration to PLAINTIFF, directs the Usher to take the note from 1ST BRIDESMAID and hand it to PLAINTIFF, who reads it, kisses it rapturously, and places it in her bosom.)

Chorus of BRIDESMAIDS.

Wear the flowers, &c.

JUDGE.

Oh never, never, never, since I joined the human race,
Saw I so exquisitely fair a face.

THE JURY (*shaking their forefingers at him*).
Ah, sly dog ! Ah, sly dog !

JUDGE (*to JURY*).
How say you, is she not designed for capture ?

FOREMAN (*after consulting with the JURY*).
We've but one word, my lord, and that is—Rapture.

PLAINTIFF (*curtseying*).
Your kindness, gentlemen, quite overpowers !

THE JURY.
We love you fondly, and would make you ours !

THE BRIDESMAIDS (*shaking their forefingers at JURY*).
Ah, sly dogs ! Ah, sly dogs !

THE JURY (*shaking their fists at DEFENDANT*).
Monster ! Monster ! dread our fury !
There's the Judge and we're the Jury !
Come substantial damages !
Substantial damages !
Damages ! dam——

USHER.
Silence in Court !

RECIT.—COUNSEL FOR PLAINTIFF.
May it please you, my lud !
Gentlemen of the jury !

ARIA.
With a sense of deep emotion,
I approach this painful case ;
For I never had a notion
That a man could be so base,
Or deceive a girl confiding,
Vows, *etcetera*, deriding.

ALL.
He deceived a girl confiding,
Vows, *etcetera*, deriding.

COUNSEL.
See my interesting client,
Victim of a heartless wile !
See the traitor all defiant
Wear a supercilious smile !
Sweetly smiled my client on him,
Coyly woo'd and gently won him.

ALL.
Sweetly smiled, &c.

COUNSEL.
Swiftly fled each honeyed hour
Spent with this unmanly male !
Camberwell became a bower,
Peckham an Arcadian Vale,
Breathing concentrated otto !—
An existence *à la* Watteau.

ALL.
Breathing concentrated otto ! &c.

COUNSEL.
Picture, then, my client naming,
And insisting on the day :
Picture him excuses framing—
Going from her far away ;
Doubly criminal to do so,
For the maid had bought her *trousseau !*

ALL.
Doubly criminal, &c.

COUNSEL (*to PLAINTIFF, who weeps*).
Cheer up, my pretty—oh cheer up !

JURY.
Cheer up, cheer up, we love you !
(COUNSEL *leads* PLAINTIFF *fondly into Witness-box, he takes a tender leave of her, and resumes his place in Court.*)
(PLAINTIFF *reels as if about to faint.*)

JUDGE.
That she is reeling
Is plain to see !

FOREMAN.
If faint your feeling
Recline on me !

She falls sobbing on to the FOREMAN's breast.)

PLAINTIFF (*feebly*).
I shall recover
If left alone.

ALL (*shaking their fists at DEFENDANT*).
Oh perjured lover,
Atone ! atone !

FOREMAN.
Just like a father
I wish to be.

(Kissing her.)

JUDGE (*approaching her*).
Or, if you'd rather
Recline on me !

(*She jumps on to Bench, sits down by the JUDGE, and falls sobbing on his breast.*)

COUNSEL.
Oh ! fetch some water
From far Cologne !

ALL.
For this sad slaughter
Atone ! atone !

JURY (*shaking fists at DEFENDANT*).
Monster, monster, dread our fury,
There's the Judge, and we're the Jury !

SONG—DEFENDANT.
Oh, gentlemen, listen, I pray,
Though I own that my heart has been ranging,
Of nature the laws I obey,
For nature is constantly changing.
The moon in her phases is found,
The time and the wind and the weather,
The months in succession come round,
And you don't find two Mondays together.
Consider the moral I pray,
Nor bring a young fellow to sorrow,
Who loves this young lady to-day,
And loves that young lady to-morrow.

BRIDESMAIDS (*rushing forward, and kneeling to JURY*).
Consider the moral, &c.
You cannot eat breakfast all day,
Nor is it the act of a sinner,
When breakfast is taken away,
To turn his attention to dinner ;
And it's not in the range of belief
To look upon him as a glutton,
Who, when he is tired of beef,
Determines to tackle the mutton.
But this I am willing to say,
If it will appease her sorrow,
I'll marry this lady to-day,
And I'll marry the other to-morrow !

BRIDESMAIDS (*rushing forward as before*).
But this he is willing to say, &c.

3

RECIT.—JUDGE.
That seems a reasonable proposition,
To which, I think, your client may agree.

COUNSEL.
But, I submit, m'lud, with all submission,
To marry two at once is Burglaree !

(*Referring to law book.*)

In the reign of James the Second,
It was generally reckoned
As a rather serious crime
To marry two wives at a time.

(*Hands book up to* JUDGE, *who reads it.*)

ALL.
Oh, man of learning !

Quartette.

JUDGE.
A nice dilemma we have here,
That calls for all our wit :

COUNSEL.
And at this stage, it don't appear
That we can settle it.

DEFENDANT.
If I to wed the girl am loth
A breach 'twill surely be—

PLAINTIFF.
And if he goes and marries both,
It counts as Burglaree !

ALL.
A nice dilemma, &c.

DUET—PLAINTIFF *and* DEFENDANT.

PLAINTIFF (*embracing him rapturously*).
I love him—I love him—with fervour unceasing,
I worship and madly adore ;
My blind adoration is ever increasing,
My loss I shall ever deplore.
Oh, see what a blessing, what love and caressing
I've lost, and remember it, pray,
When you I'm addressing, are busy assessing
The damages Edwin must pay !

DEFENDANT (*repelling her furiously*).
I smoke like a furnace—I'm always in liquor,
A ruffian—a bully—a sot ;
I'm sure I should thrash her, perhaps I should kick her,
I am such a very bad lot !
I'm not prepossessing, as you may be guessing,
She couldn't endure me a day ;
Recall my professing, when you are assessing
The damages Edwin must pay !

(*She clings to him passionately ; after a struggle, he throws her off
into arms of* COUNSEL.)

JURY.
We would be fairly acting,
But this is most distracting !
If, when in liquor, he would kick her,
That is an abatement.

PUBLIC.
She loves him, and madly adores, &c.

RECIT.—JUDGE.
The question, gentlemen—is one of liquor ;
You ask for guidance—this is my reply :
He says, when tipsy, he would thrash and kick her,
Let's make him tipsy, gentlemen, and try !

COUNSEL.
With all respect
I do object !

PLAINTIFF.
I do object !

DEFENDANT.
I don't object !

ALL.
With all respect
We do object !

JUDGE (*tossing his books and papers about.*)
All the legal furies seize you !
No proposal seems to please you,
I can't sit up here all day,
I must shortly get away.
Barristers, and you, attorneys,
Set out on your homeward journeys ;
Gentle, simple-minded usher,
Get you, if you like, to Russ*her ;*
Put your briefs upon the shelf,
I will marry her myself !

(*He comes down from Bench to floor of Court. He embraces* ANGELINA.)

FINALE.

PLAINTIFF.
Oh, joy unbounded,
With wealth surrounded,
The knell is sounded
        Of grief and woe.

COUNSEL.
With love devoted
On you he's doated,
To castle moated
        Away they go.

DEFENDANT.
I wonder whether
They'll live together
In marriage tether
        In manner true ?

USHER.
It seems to me, sir,
Of such as she, sir,
A judge is he, sir,
        And a good judge too.

CHORUS.
Oh, joy unbounded, &c.

JUDGE.
Yes, I am a Judge.

ALL.
And a good Judge too !

JUDGE.
Yes, I am a Judge.

ALL.
And a good Judge too !

JUDGE.
Though homeward as you trudge
You declare my law is fudge,
Yet of beauty I'm a judge.

ALL.
And a good Judge too !

JUDGE.
Tho' defendant is a snob—

ALL.
And a great snob too !

JUDGE.
Tho' defendant is a snob,
I'll reward him from my fob.

ALL.
So we've settled with the job,
And a good job too !

CURTAIN.

TRIAL BY JURY.
Dramatic Cantata in one Act.

Written by
W. S. GILBERT.

Composed by
ARTHUR SULLIVAN.

№ 1.

SOLO and CHORUS.

!7453.

Chappell & Co Ltd. 50, New Bond Street, London. W.– New York, Sydney

CHORUS.

Hark, the hour of ten is sound_ing; Hearts with anx_ious fears are bound_ing

Hall of Jus_tice crowds sur_round_ing, Breath_ing hope and fear— For to-day in

this a_re_na, Sum_moned by a stern sub_poe_na, Ed_win, sued by

An - ge - li - na, Short - ly will ap - pear. For to - day in this a -

Unis.

For to - day in this a - re - na, Sum - moned

- re - na, Sum - moned by a stern sub - poe - na, Ed - win, sued by An - ge - li - na, will ap -

by a stern sub - poe - na, Ed - win, sued by An - ge - li - na, Short - ly will ap - -

- pear, Ed - win, sued by An - ge - li - na, Short - ly will ap - - pear.

- pear,

Hark, the hour of ten is sounding; Hearts with anx _ ious fears are bound _ ing,

Hall of Jus _ tice crowds sur _ round _ ing, Breath _ ing hope and fear—   For to-day in

this a _ re _ na, Sum _ moned by a stern sub _ poe _ na, Ed _ win, sued by

An _ ge _ li _ na, Short _ ly will ap _ pear. Hark, the hour of ten is

sound _ ing; Hearts with anx _ ious fears are bound _ ing, Hall of Jus _ tice crowds sur _

_ round _ ing, Breath _ ing hope and fear.

6

Moderato.

Solo.—USHER.

Now, Ju _ ry _ men, hear my ad _ vice—

All kinds of

vul _ gar pre _ ju _ dice I pray you set a _ side, I pray you set a _ side:

With stern ju _ di _ cial frame of mind, From bi _ as free of ev' _ ry kind, This tri _ al must be

tried!

Si _ lence in Court!_____

Si _ lence!

Oh,

CHORUS. From bi _ as free of ev' _ ry kind, This tri _ al must be tried.

17453.

Lyrics under the staves:

lis_ten to the plain_tiff's case: Ob_serve the fea_tures of her face— The bro_ken_heart_ed

bride. Con_dole with her dis_tress of mind: From bi_as free of ev'_ry kind, This tri_al

must be tried! Si_lence in Court!_____ Si_lence! And

CHORUS. From bi_as free of ev'_ry kind This tri_al must be tried.

when a_mid the plain_tiff's shrieks, The ruf_fian_ly de_fend_ant speaks-Up_on the o_ther side; What

8

10

I'm the De _ fend _ ant!

you?

Mon _ ster, dread their

you?

Mon _ ster, dread our

dam _ a _ ges. They're the Ju _ ry, Dread their fu _ ry!

dam _ a _ ges. We're the Ju _ ry, Dread our fu _ ry!

DEFENDANT.

Hear me, hear me, if you please, These are ve _ ry strange pro _ ceed _ ings—For, per _

17453.

-mit me to re-mark, On the me-rits of my plead-ings, You're at pre-sent in the dark.

(Satirically.) That's a ve-ry true re-mark—On the me-rits of his plead-ings We're at pre-sent in the dark. Ha! ha! ho! ho! ha! ha! ho! ho!

(Defendant tunes his guitar.)

Nº 2.

SONG and CHORUS.

Allegretto. **DEFENDANT.**

1.When

first my old, old love I knew, My bo - som well'd with joy; My
joy in - ces - sant palls the sense; And love, un - chang'd will cloy; And

rich - es at her feet— I threw— I was a love - sick boy! No
she be - came a bore in - tense Un - to her love - sick boy! With

terms seem'd too — ex - tra - va - gant Up - on her to — em - ploy— I
fit - ful glim - mer burnt my flame, And I grew cold and coy,— At

2nd Verse

Just like a love - sick boy.
- no - ther's love - sick boy.

Tink, tink, tink, Tink-a-tank.

1.   2. But

L'istesso tempo.   CHORUS OF JURYMEN. (aside.)

Oh,— I was like that when a lad! A

shock-ing young scamp of a ro - ver, I be - hav'd like a re - gu-lar cad; But

that sort of thing is all o - ver. I'm__ now a res - pect - a - ble

chap And shine with a vir - tue re - splen-dent, And, there - fore, I hav - n't a

rap Of sym - pa - thy with the de - fend - ant! He shall

Allegretto.

treat us with awe, If there is - n't a flaw, Sing - ing so mer - ri - ly__

Tri - al - la - law, Trial - la - law, Trial - la - law, Sing-ing so__ mer - ri - ly__ Trial - la - law.

USHER, DEFENDANT, and FOREMAN, with SOPRANO.

Trial-la-law, Trial-la-law, Sing-ing so mer-ri-ly— Tri-al-la-law,

Trial-la-law, Trial-la-law, Sing-ing so mer-ri-ly Trial-la-law!

Moderato.
SOLO. USHER.

Si-lence in Court, si-lence in Court, and

all at-ten-tion lend. Be-hold your Judge! In due sub-mis-sion

No 3.

CHORUS and SOLO.

each de - cree _____ As sta - tute rank, And ne - ver be _____

_ Re - versed in Banc. All hail! all hail! all hail! all hail! all hail!

SOLO. JUDGE.

For these kind words ac-cept my thanks, I pray, A

Breach of Pro - mise we've to try — to - day. But first - ly, if the time you'll

Nº 4.

THE JUDGE'S SONG.

When I, good friends, was call'd to the bar, I'd an appe - tite fresh and ___ hear - ty, But I was, as many young bar - risters are An ___ im - pe - cu - nious par - ty. I'd a swallow-tail coat of a beauti - ful blue ___ A ___

brief which I bought of a boo - - by A couple of shirts and a

collar or two, And a ring that looked like a ru - by! He'd a couple of shirts and a

f CHORUS.

collar or two, And a ring that look'd like a ru - by!

2.

In Westminster Hall I danced a dance,
   Like a semi-despondent fury;
For I thought I never should hit on a chance
   Of addressing a British Jury.—
But I soon got tired of third class journeys,
   And dinners of bread and water;
So I fell in love with a rich attorney's
   Elderly, ugly daughter.

Chorus. So he fell in love, &c.

3.

The rich attorney, he jumped with joy,
   And replied to my fond professions:
"You shall reap the reward of your pluck, my boy,
   At the Bailey and Middlesex Sessions.
You'll soon get used to her looks," said he,
   "And a very nice girl you'll find her!
She may very well pass for forty-three
   In the dusk, with the light behind her!"

Chorus. She may very well pass for forty-three &c.

4.

The rich attorney was good as his word:
   The briefs came trooping gaily,
And every day my voice was heard
   At the Sessions or Ancient Bailey.
All thieves who could my fees afford
   Relied on my orations,
And many a burglar I've restored
   To his friends and his relations.

Chorus. And many a burglar he's restored &c.

you will well___ and tru - ly try.

To all of this___ we make re - ply, To all of this___ we make re - ply,

By the dull slate___ of yon - der sky: That we will well___ and

DEFENDANT. *p*   *Andante.*

COUNSEL.   They will   well   and tru - ly   try!

JUDGE. *p*

USHER.

tru - ly try.   we'll   try!

17453

Nᵒ 6.

CHORUS OF BRIDESMAIDS.

CHORUS.— THE BRIDESMAIDS.

Comes the bro-ken flow-er,— Comes the cheat-ed maid—
Though the tem-pest low - er, Rain and cloud will fade! Take, oh maid, these
po - sies: Tho' thy beau-ty rare Shame the blush-ing ro - ses—
They are pass-ing— fair, They are pass-ing fair!
Wear the flow-ers till they fade; Hap - py,

SOLO.—PLAINTIFF.

O'er the sea-son ver-nal, Time may cast a shade; Sun-shine, if e-

-ter-nal, Makes the ro-ses fade: Time may do his du-ty;

Let the thief a-lone— Win-ter hath a beau-ty, That is all his

own, That is all his own. Fair-est

days are sun and shade: I am no un-

17453.

sly dogs! We love you fond-ly and would make you, would make—you ours!

Presto furioso. JURY. *f*

Mon-ster! Mon-ster! dread our fu—ry! There's the Judge and we're the Ju—ry, Come, sub—stan—tial dam-a-ges! sub—stan-tial

dam-a-ges! dam-a-ges! dam

USHER.

Si—lence in Court!

No 8.

SONG (Defendant.)

Allegretto non troppo vivace.

Oh, gen - tle - men, lis - ten, I pray, Tho' I own that my
can - not eat break-fast all day,— Nor is it the

heart has been rang - ing, Of na - ture the laws I o -
act of a sin - ner, When break-fast is ta - ken a -

-bey, For na - ture is con - stant - ly chang-ing: The
-way, To turn his at - ten - tion to din - ner; And it's

42

17453.

CHORUS—BRIDESMAIDS.

la - dy to - mor - row! Con - si - der the mor - al we
o - ther to - mor - row! But this he is will - ing to

pray, Nor bring a young fel - low to sor - row, Who
say, If it will ap - pease her sor - row, He'll

loves this young la - dy to - day, And loves that young
mar - ry this la - dy to - day, And he'll mar - ry the

la - dy to - mor - row!   SOLO.   You
o - ther to -   - mor - row!

N⁰ 11.

seems a rea-son-able pro-po-si-tion, To which, I think, your cli-ent may a-gree!___

I sub-mit, m'lud, with all sub-mis-sion, To mar - - ry

two at once——— is Bur-gla-ree!

In the reign of James the Sec-ond, It was gen-er-al-ly reckoned As a

ra-ther se-rious crime To mar-ry two wives at a time.

CHORUS. LADIES

Oh, man of

learn-ing!

p JURY & USHER.

Oh, man of learn———ing!

SESTET AND CHORUS.

Nº 12.

50

17453.

№ 13.

DUET and CHORUS.

I love him,—I love him, with fer-vour un-ceas-ing, I wor-ship and mad-ly a-dore; My blind a-do-ra-tion is e-ver increasing, My loss I shall e-ver de-plore. Oh,— see what a bless-ing, what love and ca-ress-ing I've lost, and re-mem-ber it, pray, When you I'm ad-dress-ing, are bu-sy as-sess-ing The dam-a-ges Ed-win must pay, Yes, he must pay! I

smoke like a fur-nace—I'm al-ways in li-quor, A ruf-fian—a bul-ly—a

sot; I'm sure I should thrash her, per-haps I should kick her, I

am such a ve-ry bad__ lot! I'm__ not pre-pos-sess__-ing, as

you may be guess-ing, She could-n't en-dure me a day; Re-

-call my pro-fess__-ing, when you are as-**sess**-ing The dam-a-ges Ed-win **must**

58

17453

With all res-pect, I do ob-ject, I do ob-ject, I do ob-ject!

- ject, With all res-pect, I don't ob-ject, I don't ob-ject, I don't ob-ject!

COUNSEL and USHER.

With all res-pect, we do ob-ject, we do ob-ject, we do ob-ject!

CHORUS.

With all res-pect, we do ob-ject, we do ob-ject, we do ob-ject!

With all res-pet, we do ob-ject, we do ob-ject, we do ob-ject!

JUDGE.

All the le-gal fu-ries seize you! No pro-po-sal seems to please you,

Nº 14.

FINALE.

Allegro moderato.

PLAINTIFF.
Oh, joy un - bound - ed, With wealth sur - round - ed, The knell is sound - ed Of

COUNSEL.
grief and _woe. With love de - vot - ed, On you _he's_doat - ed, To cas - tle moat - ed A -

DEFENDANT.
way they go. I won - der whe - ther They'll live to - ge - ther, In mar - riage te - ther, In

USHER.
man - ner true? It seems to me, Sir, Of such_ as_ she, Sir, A Judge is he, Sir, And a

good judge, too!

good judge, too!

good judge, too!

good judge, too!

Though home-ward as you trudge, You de - clare my law is fudge, Yet of

good judge, too!

good judge, too!

good judge, too!

And a good judge, too!　　　And a great snob, too!

And a good judge, too!　　　No, no, no!

And a good judge, too!　　　And a great snob, too!

And a good judge, too!　　　And a great snob, too!

beau-ty I'm a judge!　　Tho' de-fen-dant is a snob,　　Tho' de-

And a good judge, too!　　　And a great snob, too!

And a good judge, too!　　　And a great snob, too!

And a good judge, too!　　　And a great snob, too!

THE PIRATES OF PENZANCE

WRITTEN BY
W. S. GILBERT

COMPOSED BY
ARTHUR SULLIVAN

VOCAL·SCORE   PIANOFORTE SOLO

LIBRETTO

THE POLICEMAN'S SONG
I AM A PIRATE KING
THE MODERN MAJOR-GENERAL
POOR WAND'RING ONE (In F and A flat)
AH! LEAVE ME NOT TO PINE ALONE (Duet)
CLIMBING OVER ROCKY MOUNTAINS (Chorus). Octavo.
VALSE (for Piano Solo)
LANCERS (for Piano Solo)
QUADRILLES (for Piano Solo)
SELECTION (for Piano Solo)
SELECTION (for Violin and Piano)

CHAPPELL & CO., LTD.,

No. 148

THE
GONDOLIERS

OR

THE KING OF BARATARIA

WRITTEN BY
W. S. GILBERT

COMPOSED BY
ARTHUR SULLIVAN

VOCAL SCORE
CHORUS EDITION

PIANOFORTE SCORE
LIBRETTO

TAKE A PAIR OF SPARKLING EYES
WHEN A MERRY MAIDEN MARRIES
KIND SIR, YOU CANNOT HAVE THE HEART
THERE LIVED A KING
IN ENTERPRISE OF MARTIAL KIND
NO POSSIBLE DOUBT WHATEVER
A REGULAR ROYAL QUEEN (Quartet). Octavo
EASY TO PLAY SELECTION (for Piano Solo)
VOCAL GEMS
SELECTION (for Piano Solo)
SELECTION (for Violin and Piano)
SELECTION (with lyrics)

CHAPPELL & CO., LTD.,

No. 3506

POPULAR COMIC OPERAS

By W. S. GILBERT and ARTHUR SULLIVAN

"THE GONDOLIERS" or "The King of Barataria"

"IOLANTHE" or "The Peer and the Peri"

"THE MIKADO" or "The Town of Titipu"

"PATIENCE" or "Bunthorne's Bride"

"THE PIRATES OF PENZANCE" or "The Slave of Duty"

"PRINCESS IDA" or "Castle Adamant"

"RUDDIGORE" or "The Witch's Curse"

"UTOPIA, LIMITED" or "The Flowers of Progress"

"TRIAL BY JURY"

"THE GRAND DUKE" or "The Statutory Duel"

"THE YEOMEN OF THE GUARD" or "The Merryman and his Maid"

*"H.M.S. PINAFORE" or "The Lass that Loved a Sailor"

*"THE SORCERER"

"HADDON HALL" by SYDNEY GRUNDY and ARTHUR SULLIVAN

"IVANHOE" by JULIAN STURGIS and ARTHUR SULLIVAN

VOCAL SCORES - PIANOFORTE SELECTIONS - LIBRETTI

EASY TO PLAY SELECTIONS - SEPARATE SONGS - VOCAL GEMS ALBUMS

PIANOFORTE SCORES - PART SONGS - CHORUSES

"THE FORESTERS," by LORD TENNYSON and ARTHUR SULLIVAN

The Songs, Choruses and Incidental Music, complete.

Selection for Piano.

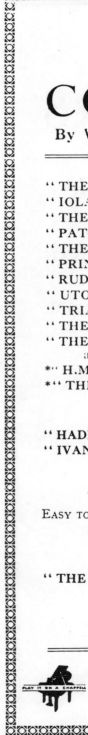 CHAPPELL & CO., LTD.,

No. 3471